New
10 –

Poems to Read on a Streetcar

NEW DIRECTIONS POETRY PAMPHLETS

#1   Susan Howe: *Sorting Facts; or, Nineteen Ways of Looking at Marker*

#2   Lydia Davis / Eliot Weinberger: *Two American Scenes*

#3   Bernadette Mayer: *The Helens of Troy, NY*

#4   Sylvia Legris: *Pneumatic Antiphonal*

#5   Nathaniel Tarn: *The Beautiful Contradictions*

#6   Alejandra Pizarnik: *A Musical Hell*

#7   H.D.: *Vale Ave*

#8   Forrest Gander: *Eiko & Koma*

#9   Lawrence Ferlinghetti: *Blasts Cries Laughter*

#10 Osama Alomar: *Fullblood Arabian*

#11 Oliverio Girondo: *Poems to Read on a Streetcar*

#12 *Fifteen Iraqi Poets* (ed., Dunya Mikhail)

Poems to Read on a Streetcar

Oliverio Girondo

Translated from the Spanish by Heather Cleary

NEW DIRECTIONS POETRY PAMPHLET #11

Some of these translations first appeared in *Two Lines: Some Kind of Beautiful Signal* and *The Literary Review.*

Cover design by Office of Paul Sahre
Interior design by Eileen Baumgartner and Erik Rieselbach
Manufactured in the United States of America
New Directions Books are printed on acid-free paper.
First published as New Directions Poetry Pamphlet #11 in 2014

Library of Congress Cataloging-in-Publication Data
Girondo, Oliverio, 1891–1967.
Poems to read on a streetcar / Oliverio Girondo ; translated by Heather Cleary.
pages cm. — (New Directions poetry pamphlet ; #11)
In English and Spanish.
ISBN 978-0-8112-2177-1 (alk. paper)
I. Cleary, Heather translator. II. Girondo, Oliverio, 1891–1967. Poems. Selections.
III. Girondo, Oliverio, 1891–1967. Poems. Selections. English. IV. Title.
PQ7797.G535A2 2014
861'.62—dc23   2013030602

10 9 8 7 6 5 4 3 2 1

New Directions Books are published for James Laughlin
by New Directions Publishing Corporation
80 Eighth Avenue, New York, NY 10011

CONTENTS

Preface   7

Veinte poemas para ser leídos en el tranvía (1922) /
Twenty Poems to Read on a Streetcar
  Café-Concert   9
  Street Note   10
  Venice   11
  Plaza   12
  Verona   13

Calcomanías (1925) / Decals
  Calle de las Sierpes   14
  Alhambra   16

Membretes (1924–1926) / Headings
  Headings   18

Espantapájaros (al alcance de todos) (1932) /
Scarecrow (Within Reach of All)
  Calligram   20
  1. "I couldn't care less if . . ."   22
  5. "Wherever we might find ourselves . . ."   24
  8. "I don't have a personality . . ."   25
  21. "May noises bore into your teeth . . ."   27

Persuasión de los días (1942) / The Persuasion of Days

    Ejecutoria de la miasma / The Miasma's Final Judgment   28

    Arena / Sand   32

    Testimonial / Testimonial   34

    "Ruiseñor del lodo" / "Mud Nightingale"   40

    Invitación al vómito / Invitation to Vomit   42

    Puedes juntar las manos / Join Your Hands   44

    Cansancio / Weariness   48

En la masmédula (1954–1963) / In the Moremarrow

    La mezcla / The Mix   52

    El puro no / The Pure No   54

    Tropos / Tropes   56

Translator's Note   61

Preface

What do you want!?! Sometimes the nerves falter ... You lose the courage to go on doing nothing—oh the weariness of never growing weary!—and you find rhythms while walking down the stairs, poems strewn in the middle of the street, poems you collect like someone picking scraps from the pavement.

What happens next is sinister. Hobby becomes occupation. We feel the shame of the pregnant. We blush if someone looks at us head on. And even worse, the occupation ends up engaging us without our knowing it, and it makes no difference if we say, "I don't want to choose because to choose is to become ossified. I don't want to have an opinion because all opinions are stupid ... even that of not having one ..."

Inevitably, we end up writing *Twenty Poems to Read on a Streetcar.*

Is it the delight of seeing ourselves humiliated? A tenderness for all we despise? I don't know. The fact is, instead of committing ourselves to their cremation, we stoop to burying these manuscripts in our desk drawer until one day, when we least expect it, question marks begin to sneak out through the keyhole.

Would an eventual success convince us of our mediocrity? Are we not stupid enough to be admired? ... Until you respond to a friend's veiled remark: "Why publish? I don't need to impress you, the rest ..."—but this friend turns out to be apocalyptic and relentless, so he replies: "Because it is vital to declare war, as you have, on the frock coat, which goes a long way in this country; on the frock coat they wear to write in Spain—when they're not writing in ruffs, cassocks, or shirtsleeves. Because it is crucial to believe, as you do, in our vernacular, since it was we Americans who oxygenized Spanish, making it a breathable language, a language for daily use, for writing about the 'American' in our everyday 'American' ..." I'm a little embarrassed to think that maybe I do have faith in our vernacular, and that maybe our vernacular might be so rude as to always be right ... I end up thinking about our country, with its hotel-room neutrality, and I'm a little embarrassed to confirm how hard it is to become attached to a hotel room ...

Publish? Publish, when even the best publish 1,071 percent more than they should? I do not have, nor do I wish to have, the blood of a statue. I do not strive to be likewise humiliated by sparrows. I do not aspire to have my tomb slathered with the drool of clichés, when the only really interesting things are systems of feeling and thought. Proof of existence!

The mundane, though: Is it not an admirable and modest manifestation of the absurd? Does cutting the ties of logic not offer the one true possibility of adventure? Why not be childish, now that we have grown weary of repeating the gestures of those buried seventy centuries ago? Why not allow for all possible means of rejuvenation? Could we not, for example, assign all responsibility to a perfect and omniscient fetish, and put our faith in prayer or in blasphemy, in the providence of paradisiacal boredom, or in the delights of damnation? What would keep us from wearing virtue and vice as though they were clean clothes, from agreeing that love is not a drug for the exclusive use of imbeciles, and from finding happiness by feigning distraction?

I, at least, in my fondness for contradiction—synonymous with life—do not renounce my right to renounce, and cast my *Twenty Poems* like a stone, smiling at the futility of my gesture.

OLIVERIO GIRONDO
(an open letter to La Púa
Paris, December 1922)

CAFÉ-CONCERT

The piston's notes follow the arc of a rocket, waver in the air, and die out before hitting the ground.

Out come a few swampy, foul-smelling eyes, teeth rotted by sugary arias, and legs that fill the stage with smoke.

The gaze of the audience is denser and has more calories than any other; it is a corrosive gaze that pierces the performers' tights and parches their skin.

There is a group of sailors hypnotized by the beacon one macquereau wears on his pinkie, a gathering of whores still dewy from the port, and an Englishman who makes fog with his eyes and his pipe.

The waitress brings me her half-bare breasts on a moonlike tray . . . breasts I would like to take home with me, to warm my feet when I get into bed.

The curtain, when it falls, looks like a curtain half raised.

Brest, August 1920

STREET NOTE

A gray family sits at a sidewalk café. A pair of cross-eyed breasts passes by, searching the tabletops for a smile. The noise of automobiles stirs the leaves on the trees. Someone stands, crucified, upon opening a fifth-floor window.

I wonder where I'll keep the kiosks, the streetlights, the passersby that come in through my eyes. I feel so full I'm afraid I might burst ... I should drop some of this deadweight to the pavement ...

As I reach the corner, my shadow breaks free and promptly throws itself under the wheels of a streetcar.

VENICE

A postcard breeze is blowing.

Terraces! Gondolas that sway like hips. Façades that weave Persian rugs on the water. Oars forever weeping.

Silence gurgles at the doorsteps, plays a pizzicato on the mooring ropes, nibbles away at the mystery of the shuttered houses.

Passing under these bridges, one takes the opportunity to blush.

Rowing in the Lagoon: dandies that carry lachrymatories filled with the iridescence of the canals in their pockets, women who have brought their lips from Vienna and Berlin to taste olive skin, and women who eat nothing but rose petals, and who have hands encrusted with serpents' eyes and the fatal jawline of D'Annunzio's heroines.

When the sun sets the city ablaze, one has no choice but to feel Nero in one's soul!

In the *piccoli canali*, gondoliers fornicate with the night, announcing their throes with a melancholy song while the moon, as she does everywhere, puffs out her chubby porter's cheeks.

I doubt that, even in this sensual city, there exist phalli more attractive or with more sudden erections than the clappers in St. Mark's campanile.

Venice, July 1921

PLAZA

The trees filter the city's clamor.

Roads that blush as they embrace the corpulent parterres. Idylls that excuse any culinary negligence. Men, anesthetized by the sun, hard to distinguish from the dead.

Life here is urban, and it is simple.

It is complicated only by:

One of those men with a wax-doll mustache that drive wet nurses wild and milk them for all they have gained by their udders.

The fireman with his hose, a *Manneken Pis*.

A woman who waves her arms like semaphores at a policeman as she feels her twins strangle each other in her belly.

Buenos Aires, December 1920

VERONA

They celebrate Mary's adultery with the Holy Dove!

A powdery rain makes the Piazza delle Erbe shine; it draws itself
up into tiny spheres that sail across the pavement and suddenly
burst, for no reason.

Between the fingers of the arcades, a dense crowd gathers its
disappointments while the band grinds out a waltz to make the
pennants turn four times and stop.

From the Virgin, who sits on her fountain as she would on a bidet,
spills water reddened by the little electric lights at her feet.

Guitars! Mandolins! Balconies without ladders and without Juliets!
Sweaty umbrellas that seem like the afterlife of a fossilized plant.
Capitals where monkeys have entertained themselves for nine
centuries by making love.

The plain, greenish, dingy sky is the same color as the soldiers'
uniforms.

Verona, July 1921

CALLE DE LAS SIERPES

For Don Ramón Gómez de la Serna

A current of backs and arms
carries us
and spills us out
under the fans,
the pipes,
the enormous spectacles
hung in the middle of the street;
lone witnesses to a vanished
race of giants.

Perched at the edge of their seats,
as if they might spring out of them
and dance,
café regulars
applaud the efforts of their waiters,
while bootblacks buff their shoes
until the listing for Sunday's bullfight
can be read in their shine.

With faces like figureheads,
and cigars acting as bowsprits,
cattle barons push their way
into drinkeries,
to draw arguments out with muletas
like matadors closing in for the kill;
leaning on bars
made to look like corrals,
they drink a toast to the spectators,

to the head of the Miura bull
that looks down on them from the wall.

Wrapped up in their capes like bullfighters,
priests duck into barber shops
to shave in four hundred mirrors at once,
but when they step back out in the street
their beards already show three days of growth.

In greenhouses
built by high society,
laziness thrives as it does nowhere else;
the members of the club gulp it down
with churros or horchata,
to run aground on armchairs
their apathy and their marionette languor.

For every two hundred and forty-seven men,
three hundred and twelve priests,
and two hundred and ninety-three soldiers,
one woman passes by.

Seville, April 1923

ALHAMBRA

For Margarita Nelken

The fountains spray
a lassitude
that just barely allows us to reflect
with our pores, our cerebellum, and our nose.

Absinthe pools
in which the stone lace of the arches
has been left to soak!

Chambers in which light takes on
all the sweet sensuousness
that it does
between the parted lips of a woman!

As verbose as la Celestina,
the guides
usher the ladies toward the harem
so they might blush to hear
the fountains' gossip as they pass,
and be overcome by nostalgia
as they look out across Albaicín,
and listen to the Mozarabic song
the city sings, soft and low,
to this very day.

With the neck and movements of praying mantises,
English women compose their palette
of the gray of their Londoner's eyes

and the incarnate desperation of their virginity,
and, as though looking in a mirror,
they reproduce,
with postcard exaltations,
rooms filled with wistful, pillowed memories
and shadows as purple as rings under eyes.

In the Lindaraja observatory,
the visitors shiver when they realize
that the columns
are of the same pallor and girth
as the arms of the sultan's favored wife,
and in the baths
they sniff the air
trying to catch
the scent of odalisque flesh,
flesh with the same consistency and flavor
as gumdrops.

Shutters burnished
by the countless eyes
that have looked through them!

Walls that have a temperature of ninety-eight degrees in the shade
beneath their crocheted blouses!

Without fail,
each time we leave
the Alhambra
it is as though we were coming back
from a romantic liaison.

Granada, March 1923

HEADINGS

Musically, the clarinet is a far richer instrument than the dictionary.

There is no better critic than our own desk drawer.

The silence of El Greco's canvases is ascetic, Maeterlinckian; it disorients his subjects, sets their mouths off-balance, shifts their gaze, and dissolves their noses.

There comes a time when we aspire to write something worse.

Let us expose another kind of onanism: that of raising the flag every five minutes.

The Clothed Maja is more naked than *The Naked Maja*.

The worst enemy of art is Art! A fetish over which preside, on their knees, those who are not artists.

Murillo's virgins?
As virgins, too womanly.
As women, too virginal.

A book should be made like a watch and sold like a sausage.

The baroque needed to cross the Atlantic in search of the tropics and the jungle in order to acquire the sincere and fortuitous naïveté it boasts in America.

The remarkable thing is not that van Gogh cut off an ear but rather that he kept one.

Certain they know where it resides, there is always a hurried and impatient crowd running around in search of poetry, but when they arrive where they were told it could be found, they are always met with the same response: It moved.

We aspire to plagiarize no one, not even ourselves, and to be different every time, renewing ourselves with each poem, but as we go along amassing our stark or florid bodies of work, we should acknowledge that over the course of our existence we have written one poem, and one poem only.

Yo   no   sé   nada
Tú   no   sabes   nada
Ud.   no   sabe   nada
Él   no   sabe   nada
Ellos no   saben nada
Ellas no   saben nada
Uds. no   saben nada
Nosotros no sabemos nada

La desorientación de mi generación tiene su explicación en la dirección de nuestra educación, cuya idealización de la acción era —¡sin discusión!—una mistificación, en contradicción con nuestra propensión a la meditación, a la contemplación y a la masturbación.
(Gutural, lo más guturalmente
que se pueda.) Creo que creo
en lo que creo que no creo.
Y creo que no creo en
lo que creo que creo.

"Cantar de las ranas"

¡Y	¡Y	¿A		¿A	¡Y	¡Y
su	**ba**	llí		llá	**su**	ba
bo	**jo**	es		es	**bo**	jo
las	**las**	tá?		ta?	**las**	las
es	**es**	¡A		¡A	**es**	es
ca	**ca**	quí		cá	**ca**	ca
le	**le**	no		no	**le**	le
ras	**ras**	es		es	**ras**	ras
arri	**ba**	tá		tá	**arri**	aba
ba!…	**jo!…**	!…		!…	**ba!…**	jo!…

I   know   nothing
You   know   nothing
He   knows   nothing
She   knows   nothing
It   knows   nothing
They   know   nothing
We   know   nothing

The disorientation of my generation finds its explanation in our education, whose idealization of action was—without question!—a mystification, a contradiction of our natural predilection for meditation, for contemplation, and for masturbation.

(Guttural, as guttural as can
be.) I believe I believe what
I believe I don't believe. And
I don't believe I believe
what I believe I believe.

"Frog song"

```
        ¡A   ¡A   Is        Is   ¡A   ¡A
       nd   nd   it        it   nd   nd
       up   do   he       the   up   do
      the   wn   re?      re?  the   wn
   st   the   No,         No,   st   the
 airs   st   not          not  airs   st
 I     airs   he          the   I   airs
 go   I go   re            re   go   I go
 !...  !...  !...               !...  !...  !...
```

1.

I couldn't care less if a woman has breasts like magnolias or dried figs; skin as soft as a peach or as rough as sandpaper. I assign zero importance to whether her breath in the morning is more like aphrodisia or insecticide. I am perfectly capable of enduring a nose that would win first prize in a carrot competition, but in *this* I will not be swayed: I cannot forgive, under any circumstances, an inability to fly. If they don't know how to fly, they're wasting their time trying to seduce me!

This was the reason—and no other—that I fell so madly in love with María Luisa.

What did it matter that her lips came in installments and that her sex was sulfuric? What did I care about her webbed toes and her glances of guarded judgment?

María Luisa was an absolute feather!

She was flying at the first light of day: from the bedroom to the kitchen, from the dining room to the pantry. She flew as she drew my bath and ironed my shirt. She flew as she shopped and did her chores.

How impatiently would I wait for her to fly back from this or that trip through the neighborhood! There, in the distance, lost among the clouds: a little pinkish speck. "María Luisa! María Luisa!" ... and then there she was, wrapping me in her feathered legs and lifting me into flight.

For miles, we soared in silent caresses that brought us near paradise; we would nest for hours inside a cloud, like angels, until a spasm would suddenly bring us crashing back to earth in the corkscrew plummet of a dead leaf.

What a treat it is to hold a woman so light ... even if, from time to time, she makes us see stars! How indulgent, to spend your days in the clouds and your nights in a single, continuous flight!

After knowing an ethereal woman, what attraction could a terrestrial one possibly have? Is there a difference between living with a cow and living with a woman whose buttocks are two and a half feet from the ground?

I, at least, am unable to comprehend the appeal of a pedestrian woman and, no matter how hard I try, cannot so much as imagine making love unless it is in flight.

5.

Wherever we might find ourselves, at any hour of the day or night, there they are: relatives! Distant relations, perhaps, but with a lineage identical to our own.

That cat sitting in the window licking its haunches? ... The same eyes as Aunt Caroline! The carriage horse stumbling across the pavement? ... The yellowish teeth of my grandfather José María!

A fine thing, finding relatives at every turn! Sharing blood with those who want to bleed you dry!

And what is worse, these bonds of consanguinity are not limited to the zoological. The certainty of the common origin of species expands our memory to the point that the borders of the kingdoms begin to blur and we feel ourselves as close to crystals and grains as we do to herbivores. Seven, seventy, or seven hundred generations end up resembling one another in our eyes, and we realize that (as different as they might look) we have as much carrot as camel in us.

After galloping nine leagues across the pampa, we sit down to a steaming pot of stew. Three bites ... and we feel a lump in our throats. A geological age ago, might we not have shared a father with that squash? Garbanzo beans taste divine, but what if it turned out that we were devouring our own brothers?

As our existence becomes more and more confused with the existence of all that surrounds us, the fear of harming a member of our family grows more and more intense. Bit by bit, our lives become a continuous series of shocks. The regret that gnaws at our conscience begins to hinder even the most essential functions of our body and spirit. Before moving an arm or stretching a leg, we think of the effects this gesture might have on our kin. With each passing day it becomes more difficult to eat and to breathe, until finally we are forced to choose, resigning ourselves to commit every incest, every murder, every cruelty, or to be, simply and humbly, a victim of the family.

8.

I don't have a personality. I am a cocktail, an amalgam, a procession of personalities.

In me, personality is a case of psychological boils in a constant state of eruption—not half an hour goes by that a new personality doesn't surface.

Since I have known me, the accumulation has been such that my house looks like the waiting room of a fashionable palm reader. There are personalities everywhere: in the foyer, in the hall, in the kitchen, even in the WC ...

Impossible to find a moment of peace, of rest! Impossible to know which is the real one!

Though I am forced to live in total promiscuity with all of them, I am not entirely sure they are mine.

What do they have to do with me—I wonder—these unspeakable personalities that would make a butcher blush? Must I allow myself to be identified with, for example, the withered pederast who never had the courage to actually become one, or the cretin whose smile is enough to freeze a train?

The fact that they all live inside me is enough to make me sick with indignation. Since I cannot ignore their existence, I'd like to make them hide in the deepest recesses of my brain. But they're so petulant ... so selfish ... so tactless ...

Even the least important personalities put on airs fit for an ocean liner. All of them, without exception, believe they have the right to show Olympian disdain for the rest and so, naturally, there are fights, all sorts of conflicts, endless arguments. Instead of being agreeable— no, sir!—each one tries to impose its will, not taking the opinions and tastes of the others into account. If one of them gives me a good laugh, there's another waiting in the wings to propose a little stroll through the cemetery. As soon as this one tells me to sleep with all the women in the city, that one insists on showing me the virtue of abstinence, and while one of them goes wild at night and won't let me fall asleep until the small hours, another wakes me at dawn and demands that I rise with the sun.

My life is thus the gestation of possibilities that are never realized, an explosion of contradictory forces that clash and destroy one another. Even the slightest decision causes a huge disturbance; before performing even the most insignificant act, I have to get so many personalities to agree that I prefer to throw my hands up and wait for them to wear themselves out arguing about what they should do with me, in order to have, at least, the satisfaction of telling them all to go to hell.

21.

May noises bore into your teeth like a dentist's drill, and may your memory be filled with rust, befouled odors, and broken words.

May a spider's leg grow from each of your pores; may you be able to eat only used decks of cards; and may exhaustion reduce you, like a steamroller, to the thickness of your portrait.

When you step into the street, may even the lampposts chase you off with kicks; may an overwhelming compulsion lead you to bow down before garbage pails; and may everyone in the city mistake you for a urinal.

Whenever you try to say "I love you," may it come out sounding like "fried fish," and may your own hands try to strangle you every now and then. Instead of your cigarette, may it be you that you toss in the spittoon.

May your wife cheat on you constantly, even with mailboxes; when she lies down beside you, may she turn into a leech; and—after birthing a raven—may she bear you a wrench.

May your family entertain itself by so disfiguring your skeleton that when mirrors see you they kill themselves in disgust; may your only amusement be installing yourself in the waiting rooms of dentists dressed as a crocodile; and may you fall so madly in love with a safe-deposit box that you cannot, even for an instant, resist licking its latch.

EJECUTORIA DEL MIASMA

Este clima de asfixia que impregna los pulmones
de una anhelante angustia de pez recién pescado.
Este hedor adhesivo y errabundo,
que intoxica la vida
y nos hunde en viscosas pesadillas de lodo.
Este miasma corrupto,
que insufla en nuestros poros
apetencias de pulpo,
deseos de vinchuca,
no surge,
ni ha surgido
de estos conglomerados de sucia hemoglobina,
cal viva,
soda cáustica,
hidrógeno,
pis úrico,
que infectan los colchones,
los techos,
las veredas,
con sus almas cariadas,
con sus gestos leprosos.

Este olor homicida,
rastrero,
ineludible,
brota de otras raíces,
arranca de otras fuentes.

THE MIASMA'S FINAL JUDGMENT

This air of asphyxia that saturates our lungs
with the plaintive anguish of a freshly caught fish.
This roving and tenacious stench,
that poisons life
and drowns us in viscous nightmares of mud.
This venal fog
that insufflates our pores
with octopus cravings,
bedbug desires,
does not come,
has never come,
from these aggregates of filthy hemoglobin,
living quicklime,
lye,
hydrogen,
uric piss,
that contaminate mattresses,
ceilings,
sidewalks,
with their putrid souls,
their leprous gestures.

This homicidal fetor,
contemptible,
inescapable,
sprouts from other roots,
spurts from other wells.

A través de años muertos,
de atardeceres rancios,
de sepulcros gaseosos,
de cauces subterráneos,
se ha ido aglutinando con los jugos pestíferos,
los detritus hediondos,
las corrosivas vísceras,
las esquirlas podridas que dejaron el crimen,
la idiotez purulenta,
la iniquidad sin sexo,
el gangrenoso engaño;
hasta surgir al aire,
expandirse en el viento
y tornarse corpóreo;
para abrir las ventanas,
penetrar en los cuartos,
tomarnos del cogote,
empujarnos al asco,
mientras grita su inquina,
su aversión,
su desprecio,
por todo lo que allana la acritud de las horas,
por todo lo que alivia la angustia de los días.

Through lifeless years
and rancid dusks,
through gaseous tombs
and underground channels,
it's gone along, swelling with noxious fluids,
stinking detritus,
and caustic entrails,
rotten splinters from the scene of the crime,
purulent idiocy,
sexless iniquity,
gangrenous deception;
until it rises into the air,
stretches out on the wind,
and gives itself form;
to open windows,
penetrate rooms,
grab us by the neck,
thrust us toward repulsion,
as it shrieks its loathing,
its aversion,
its disdain,
for all that tempers the rancor of hours,
for all that relieves the anguish of days.

ARENA

Arena,
y más arena,
y nada más que arena.

De arena el horizonte.
El destino de arena.
De arena los caminos.
El cansancio de arena.
De arena las palabras.
El silencio de arena.

Arena de los ojos con pupilas de arena.
Arena de las bocas con los labios de arena.
Arena de la sangre de las venas de arena.

Arena de la muerte ...
De la muerte de arena.

¡Nada más que de arena!

SAND

Sand,
and more sand,
and nothing but sand.

Sand horizon.
Destiny of sand.
Sand paths.
Weariness of sand.
Sand words.
Silence of sand.

The sand of eyes with pupils of sand.
The sand of mouths with lips of sand.
The sand of blood from veins of sand.

The sand of death ...
Of a death by sand.

Nothing but sand!

TESTIMONIAL

Allí están,
allí estaban
las trashumantes nubes,
la fácil desnudez del arroyo,
la voz de la madera,
los trigales ardientes,
la amistad apacible de las piedras.

Allí la sal,
los juncos que se bañan,
el melodioso sueño de los sauces,
el trino de los astros,
de los grillos,
la luna recostada sobre el césped,
el horizonte azul,
¡el horizonte!
con sus briosos tordillos por el aire …

¡Pero no!
Nos sedujo lo infecto,
la opinión clamorosa de las cloacas,
los vibrantes eructos de onda corta,
el pasional engrudo,
las circuncisas lenguas de cemento,
los poetas de moco enternecido,
los vocablos,
las sombras sin remedio.

TESTIMONIAL

There they are,
there they were
the migratory clouds,
the stream's easy bareness,
the voice of the wood,
the wheat fields ablaze,
the gentle company of stones.

There, the salt,
the tide-washed reeds,
the willow's melodic slumber
the call of the stars,
of the crickets,
the moon, lying in the grass,
the blue horizon,
the horizon!
its dapple grays at full gallop against the sky ...

But no!
We were seduced by the infected,
by the clamorous voice of the sewers,
resonant belches of shortwave,
passions in papier-mâché,
circumcised tongues of concrete,
by snot-caressing poets,
by words,
incurable shadows.

Y aquí estamos:
exangües,
más pálidos que nunca;
como tibios pescados corrompidos
por tanto mercader y ruido muerto;
como mustias acelgas digeridas
por la preocupación y la dispepsia;
como resumideros ululantes
que toman el tranvía
y bostezan
y sudan
sobre el carbón, la cal, las telarañas;
como erectos ombligos con pelusa
que se rascan las piernas y sonríen,
bajo los cielorrasos
y las mesas de luz
y los felpudos;
llenos de iniquidad y de lagañas,
llenos de hiel y tics a contrapelo,
de histrionismos madeja,
yarará,
mosca muerta;
con el cráneo repleto de aserrín escupido,
con las venas pobladas de alacranes filtrables,
con los ojos rodeados de pantanosas costas
y paisajes de arena,
nada más que de arena.
Escoria entumecida de enquistados complejos
y cascarrientos labios
que se olvida del sexo en todas partes,
que confunde el amor con el masaje,
la poesía con la congoja acidulada,
los misales con los libros de caja.
Desolados engendros del azar y el hastío,

And here we are:
drained,
paler than ever,
like tepid fish rotted
by commerce and noise;
like withered leaves of chard digested
by disquiet and dyspepsia;
like gurgling cesspools
that ride the streetcars
and yawn
and sweat
on coal, quicklime, cobwebs;
like downy erect navels
that scratch their legs and smile,
under ceilings
and nightstands
and doormats;
full of sin and secretions,
full of bile and irritating tics,
of tightly wound histrionics,
vipers,
wolves in sheep's clothing
with crania full of regurgitated sawdust,
granular scorpions coursing through their veins,
with eyes surrounded by marshy coastlines
and landscapes of sand,
of nothing but sand.
The turgid dregs of tumoral neuroses,
and cracked lips
that leaves its genitals lying around,
that confuses love with a massage,
poetry with acrid malaise,
the missals with a book of checks.
The forsaken spawn of chance and tedium,

con la carne exprimida
por los bancos de estuco y tripas de oro,
por los dedos cubiertos de insaciables ventosas,
por los viejos gargajos de cuello almidonado,
por cuantos mingitorios con trato de excelencia
explotan las tinieblas,
ordeñan las cascadas,
la adulcorada caña,
la sangre oleaginosa de los falsos caballos,
sin orejas,
sin cascos,
ni florecido esfínter de amapola,
que los llevan al hambre,
a empeñar la esperanza,
a vender los ovarios,
a cortar a pedazos sus adoradas madres,
a ingerir los infundios que pregonan las lámparas,
los hilos tartamudos,
los babosos escuerzos que tienen la palabra,
y hablan,
hablan,
hablan,
ante las barbas próceres,
o verdes redomones de bronce que no mean,
ante las multitudes
que desde un sexto piso
podrán ser parecidas al caviar envasado,
aunque de cerca apestan:
a sudor sometido,
a cama trasnochada,
a sacrificio inútil,
a rencor estancado,
a pis en cuarentena,
a rata muerta.

with flesh wrung dry
by stucco banks and bowels of gold,
by fingers covered with insatiable suckers,
by the time-worn gurglings of starched collars,
by countless urinals bearing seals of quality,
they exploit the half-light,
milk the waterfalls,
the sweetened cane,
the oily blood of fake horses,
without ears,
without helmets,
or the blossoming poppy sphincter
that drives them toward starvation,
makes them pawn their hope,
sell their ovaries,
cut their precious mothers to pieces,
ingest the slander spread by streetlamps,
by stuttering threads,
by slobbering toads with license to speak,
and they talk,
and talk,
and talk,
before distinguished beards,
and greenish-bronze wild horses that don't piss,
before the masses
which, from a sixth-floor window,
could pass for packaged caviar,
even though up close they stink:
of stifled sweat,
of unslept-in beds,
of useless sacrifice,
of stagnant rancor,
of piss held in,
of dead rats.

"RUISEÑOR DEL LODO"

Corbière

¿Por qué bajas los párpados?

Ya sé que estás desnudo,
pero puedes mirarme con los ojos tranquilos.
Los días nos enseñan que la fealdad no existe.

Tu vientre de canónigo
y tus manos reumáticas,
no impiden que te pases la noche en los pantanos,
mirando las estrellas,   .
mientras cantas y oficias tus misas gregorianas.

Frecuenta cuanto quieras el farol y el alero.
Me entretiene tu gula
y tu supervivencia entre seres recientes:
"parvenus" de la tierra.

Pero has de perdonarme
si no te doy la mano.
Tú tienes sangre fría.
Yo, demasiada fiebre.

"MUD NIGHTINGALE"

Corbière

Why do you lower your eyes?

Yes, I know you're naked,
but you can look at me untroubled.
Time has shown us there is no such thing as ugliness.

Your sacerdotal belly
and your arthritic hands
don't keep you from spending your nights in the swamps,
gazing at the stars,
as you intone your Gregorian mass.

Visit our eaves and streetlamps as often as you like.
I'm amused by your gluttony
and your resilience among recent beings,
earthy parvenus.

But you'll have to forgive me
if I don't offer you my hand.
Your blood is cold.
Mine, far too hot.

INVITACIÓN AL VÓMITO

Cúbrete el rostro
y llora.
Vomita.
¡Si!
Vomita,
largos trozos de vidrio,
amargos alfileres,
turbios gritos de espanto,
vocablos carcomidos;
sobre este purulento desborde de inocencia,
ante esta nauseabunda iniquidad sin cauce,
y esta castrada y fétida sumisión cultivada
en flatulentos caldos de terror y de ayuno.

Cúbrete el rostro
y llora ...
pero no te contengas.
Vomita.
¡Si!
Vomita,
ante esta paranoica estupidez macabra,
sobre este delirante cretinismo estentóreo
y esta senil orgia de egoísmo prostático:
lacios coágulos de asco,
macerada impotencia,
rancios jugos de hastío,
trozos de amarga espera ...
horas entrecortadas por relinchos de angustia.

INVITATION TO VOMIT

Cover your face
and cry.
Vomit.
Yes!
Vomit,
long shards of glass,
bitter needles,
murky shrieks of shock,
corroded words;
at this purulent torrent of innocence,
over this nauseating boundless iniquity,
this fetid, castrated submission cultivated
in flatulent broths of fear and fasting.

Cover your face
and cry ...
but don't hold it in.
Vomit.
Yes!
Vomit,
at this macabre paranoid stupidity,
over this delirious vociferous cretinism,
this senile orgy of prostate egotism:
flaccid clots of revulsion,
macerated impotence,
the rancid juices of disgust,
shards of bitter postponement ...
hours shot through with bleats of pain.

PUEDES JUNTAR LAS MANOS

La gente dice:
Polvo,
Sideral,
Funerario,
y se queda tranquila,
contenta,
satisfecha.

Pero escucha ese grillo,
esa brizna de noche,
de vida enloquecida.

Ahora es cuando canta.
Ahora
       y no mañana.
Precisamente ahora.
          Aquí.
             A nuestro lado ...
como si no pudiera cantar en otra parte.

¿Comprendes?
      Yo tampoco.
           Yo no comprendo nada.

No tan sólo tus manos son un puro milagro.
Un traspiés,
un olvido,
y acaso fueras mosca,
lechuga,
cocodrilo.

JOIN YOUR HANDS

The people say:
Dust,
Celestial,
Sepulchral,
and are left calm,
mollified,
satisfied.

But listen to this cricket,
that wisp of night,
of a lunatic existence.

Now is the time for it to sing.
Now
        and not tomorrow.
Right now.
                Here.
                At our side ...
as if there were nowhere else it could.

Do you understand?
        Me neither.
                I don't understand a thing.

It's not just your hands that are pure miracle.
A misstep,
a lost thought,
and you might have been a fly,
lettuce,
a crocodile.

Y después ...
esa estrella.
      No preguntes.
            ¡Misterio!

El silencio.
      Tu pelo.

Y el fervor,
la aquiescencia
del universo entero,
para lograr tus poros,
      esa ortiga,
            esa piedra.

Puedes juntar las manos.
      Amputarte las trenzas.

      Yo daré mientras tanto tres vueltas de carnero.

And then ...
that star.
     Don't ask.
         Mystery!

The silence.
     Your hair.

And the passion,
the acquiescence
of the whole universe,
it took to make your pores,
     that nettle,
         that rock.

Join your hands.
     Amputate your braids.

     In the meantime I'll turn three somersaults.

CANSANCIO

Cansado.
¡Sí!
Cansado
de usar un solo bazo,
dos labios,
veinte dedos,
no sé cuántas palabras,
no sé cuantos recuerdos,
grisáceos,
fragmentarios.

Cansado,
muy cansado
de este frío esqueleto,
tan púdico,
tan casto,
que cuando se desnude
no sabrá si es el mismo
que usé mientras vivía.

Cansado.
¡Sí!
Cansado
por carecer de antenas,
de un ojo en cada omóplato
y de una cola autentica,
alegre
desatada,
y no este rabo hipócrita,
degenerado,
enano.

WEARINESS

Weary.
Yes!
Weary
of using just one spleen,
two lips,
twenty digits,
however many words,
however many memories,
grayish,
fragmentary.

Weary,
so weary
of this frigid skeleton,
so modest,
so chaste,
that when it undresses
I won't recognize it
as the one I used in life.

Weary.
Yes!
Weary
of a life without antennas,
an eye in each shoulder blade,
or a real tail,
happy,
unrestrained,
not this hypocrite stump,
degenerate,
dwarfish.

Cansado,
sobre todo,
de estar siempre conmigo,
de hallarme cada día,
cuando termina el sueño,
allí, donde me encuentre,
con las mismas narices
y con las mismas piernas;
como si no deseara
esperar la rompiente con un cutis de playa,
ofrecer, al rocío, dos senos de magnolia,
acariciar la tierra con un vientre de oruga,
y vivir, unos meses, adentro de una piedra.

Weary,
more than anything,
of always being with myself,
of running into me day after day,
at the end of my slumber,
there, wherever I find myself
it's with the same nose
and the same legs;
as if I didn't wish
to meet the waves in the skin of a beach,
offer, to the dew, two magnolia breasts,
caress the earth with a caterpillar's belly,
and live, for a few months, inside a stone.

LA MEZCLA

No sólo
el fofo fondo
los ebrios lechos légamos telúricos entre fanales senos
y sus líquenes
no sólo el solicroo
las prefugas
lo impar ido
el ahonde
el tacto incauto solo
los acordes abismos de los órganos sacros del orgasmo
el gusto al riesgo en brote
al rito negro al alba con su esperezo lleno de gorriones
ni tampoco el regosto
los suspiritos sólo
ni el fortuito dial sino
o los autosondeos en pleno plexo trópico
ni las exellas menos ni el endédalo
sino la viva mezcla
la total mezcla plena
la pura impura mezcla que me merme los machimbres el almamasa
    tensa las tercas hembras tuercas
la mezcla
sí
la mezcla con que adherí mis puentes

THE MIX

Not only
the doughy depths
the drunken mud earthy sludge between beacons breasts
and its algae
not only the solocroak
the prefugues
the un borne
the fathoming
the lone rushed touch
the harmonic abyss of sacred organs of orgasm
the taste of risk welling
into the black rites of dawn with its sparrowous throes
or the craving more
the little sighs
the fortunous wheel
the selfsoundings of the tropic plexus
or the former-hers and less even the inlabyrinths
but the living mix
the utter total mix
the pure impure mix that melts my joinings my soulmass shapes hard
     nuts to bolts
the mix
yes
the mix by which I built my bridges

EL PURO NO

El no
el no inóvulo
el no nonato
el noo
el no poslodocosmos de impuros ceros noes que noan noan noan
y nooan
y plurimono noan al morbo amorfo noo
no démono
no deo
sin son sin sexo ni órbita
el yerto inóseo noo en unisolo amódulo
sin poros ya sin nódulo
ni yo ni fosa ni hoyo
el macro no ni polvo
el no más nada todo
el puro no
sin no

THE PURE NO

The no
the inovulate no
the nonatal no
the noo
the postprotocosmic no of impure no zeros that no no no
and nooo
and multimono no to the morbid amorphous nooo
demonate no
te deus no
soundless sexless courseless
the rigid unossified nooo in nonmodular oneonly
the nodeless poreless no
no I no hole no hollow
the macro ashless no
the most nothing no
the pure no
no less

TROPOS

Toco
toco poros
amarras
calas toco
teclas de nervios
muelles
tejidos que me tocan
cicatrices
cenizas
trópicos vientres toco
solos solos
resacas
estertores
toco y mastoco
y nada

Prefiguras de ausencia
inconsistentes tropos
qué tú
qué qué
qué quenas
qué hondonadas
qué máscaras
qué soledades huecas
qué sí qué no
qué sino que me destempla el toque
qué reflejos
qué fondos
qué materiales brujos

TROPES

I touch
I poke pores
moorings
touch little inlets
neural nodes
landings
tissues that touch me
scars
ash
I touch tropic paunches
lonely only
undertows
throes
I palpate and paleate
and nothing

Harbingers of absence
insubstantial tropes
what you
what what
what whistles
what chasms
what masks
what hollow solitudes
what whatever
what if not unhinged by a touch
what reflections
what depths
what witchy elements

qué llaves
qué ingredientes nocturnos
qué fallebas heladas que no abren
qué nada toco
en todo

what keys
what midnight materials
what latches frozen shut
what naught I touch
in all

Translator's Note

Certain they know where it resides, there is always a hurried and impatient crowd running around in search of poetry, but when they arrive where they were told it could be found, they are always met with the same response: It moved.
—Oliverio Girondo, from "Headings"

Oliverio Girondo (1890–1967) played a fundamental role in the development of the Latin American avant-garde as he shifted nimbly between prose and verse, the grotesque and the sublime, winding his way toward a complex, playful, poetic language all his own.

As a young man in Buenos Aires, the poet cut a deal with his family: He would attend law school as was expected of him, but only on the condition that his parents underwrite several extended trips through Europe. Girondo's first collection, *Veinte poemas para ser leídos en el tranvía* (Twenty Poems to Read on a Streetcar, 1922), is a series of snapshots from these travels that treats poetry not as a pleasure reserved for the study or the salon but instead as something found in the most mundane public settings, "strewn in the middle of the street" amid the bustle of city life. Its preface, a letter written to the members of La Púa ("the spike")—a group that gathered in Buenos Aires and Paris in the early 1920s to discuss art and literature—also introduces this pamphlet. Though the missive hits a shrill note at times, its censure of creative stagnation is key to understanding the constant search for new forms that marks Girondo's oeuvre.

Jorge Luis Borges, in his review of *Calcomanías* (Decals, 1925), says with a wink that Girondo is "a violent man" who "stares at something for a while, then suddenly slaps it in the face." The poet's penchant for disruptive metaphors and images, the bracing and irreverent slaps in the face he lets loose throughout his creative life, is indeed evident in these early collections, though there is also a marked sense of affection for the host of figures that populate their pages. From the pair of "cross-eyed breasts" searching the tabletops of a sidewalk café for a smile, to Andalusian priests "wrapped up in their capes like bullfighters," the flat surface of urban anonymity shatters into a string of vivid images bound to the personal experiences of the poet. "Calle de las Sierpes," which takes its name from a busy commercial street in the heart of Seville, is dedicated to Ramón Gómez de la Serna, a prominent figure of the Spanish avant-garde and dear friend to Girondo, whose *greguerías*—humorous aphorisms—inspired the poet's *Membretes* (Headings), published in the magazine *Martín Fierro* between 1924 and 1926.

In 1932, following his own dictum that "a book should be made like a watch and sold like a sausage," Girondo released his next collection, *Espantapájaros (al alcance de todos)* [Scarecrow (Within Reach of All)], amid a publicity spectacle unlike any seen before in Buenos Aires. He hired a funeral carriage and two drivers in formal attire to cart a giant papier-mâché scarecrow in a top hat and monocle around the city while attractive young women sold copies of the book from a storefront on a busy downtown street. The print run sold out almost immediately. The collection, a return to prose poems, is introduced by a calligram in the shape of a scarecrow whose head is composed of a full declension of the phrase "to know nothing" and whose viscera assert, "I believe I believe what I believe I don't believe." This is Girondo's most playful and bawdy collection, though the affinity with the natural world that he explores here provides a bridge between his early and later work.

The next collection to appear, *Persuasión de los días* (The Persuasion of Days, 1942), marks a significant shift in the tone of Girondo's poetry. A triptych in free verse, the collection opens with "A Shoreless Flight," an aerial tour of a city made up of desolate streets and buildings in disrepair. In "Testimonial" Girondo inveighs against an urban culture that leaves its inhabitants "drained, / paler than ever, / like tepid fish rotted / by commerce and noise." The disillusionment and estrangement that evoke—at times subtly, at times explicitly—the violence of the Second World War gradually shift toward a unique experience of language the poet associates with the natural realm. As though the vitality of language, too, had been threatened by the human suffering described in its opening pages, the final section of *Persuasión* finds Girondo pushing the boundaries of poetic expression.

A year after the publication of *Persuasión*, Girondo and his long-time partner Norah Lange, an Argentine writer of Scandinavian descent, were married and spent several months traveling around South America on a honeymoon that brought them into contact with Oswald de Andrade, Jules Supervielle, Gabriela Mistral, and Mário de Andrade. These writers, along with Federico García Lorca and Pablo Neruda—who would later pen an homage to the poet—would remain fixtures in Girondo's social and creative life.

Girondo brings the linguistic play that first appears in *Persuasión* to its upper limit in *En la masmédula* (In the Moremarrow), published in various configurations between 1954 and 1963. Here the function of language is no longer simply to convey ideas or images—though this function is not abandoned entirely—it also becomes an experience in which phonetic resonances create a verbal synesthesia, a kaleidoscopic confusion of word and sound, in which one term follows or is combined with another as much for the phonetic affinity between the two as for the semantic connotations of the phrase. With its neologisms and its complex rhythms, *En la masmédula* is a collection that is felt physically as much as it is read, endowing the work with a deeply personal, almost hermetic air.

Unwilling to join that hurried and impatient crowd, Girondo remained dedicated to the campaign against poetic ossification that he launched in his letter to La Púa in 1922, pressing constantly into new formal and linguistic territories. The works selected for this pamphlet are meant to reflect this breadth, as well as the conceptual and symbolic depth, of his creative production. Due to reasons of space, a few important texts—the 1924 manifesto of *Martín Fierro* and

Campo nuestro (1946), a striking paean to the Argentine countryside, among them—had to be left out and await a larger edition.

Finally, this book would not exist at all were it not for the help of Susana Lange of the Girondo estate, who has been so generous with her support and her expertise; Eliot Weinberger and Richard Sieburth, who encouraged and shaped this project in its infancy and who shepherd it still; the PEN/Heim Translation Fund; and Jeffrey Yang, whose editorial guidance and enthusiasm for Girondo's poetry have been most appreciated throughout.

HEATHER CLEARY